Rupture, Light

poems by

Melissa Reeser Poulin

Finishing Line Press
Georgetown, Kentucky

Rupture, Light

Copyright © 2019 by Melissa Reeser Poulin
ISBN 978-1-63534-818-7 First Edition
All rights reserved under International and Pan-American Copyright Conventions. No part of this book may be reproduced in any manner whatsoever without written permission from the publisher, except in the case of brief quotations embodied in critical articles and reviews.

ACKNOWLEDGMENTS

Thank you to the editors of the following journals and anthologies in which these poems appear, some in earlier versions:

"Translations," "Yellow," "Imsland," "The Prayer," and "The Seeker," *Ruminate Magazine.*
"Nullus Partus," *Taos Journal of International Poetry & Art*
"At the Roadside Rock and Gem Store," *basalt*
"Working from Home," *Water~Stone Review*
"Snow and Ashes," *M Review*
"Bean Saving," *Mothers Always Write*
"An Incomplete Alphabet," *Ekphrastic Review*
"My Daughter Plays with Water," *Milkteeth* (forthcoming from Hermeneutic Chaos)

Publisher: Leah Maines
Editor: Christen Kincaid
Cover Art: *Glow Over the Trees*, Yared Nigussu, www.yarednigussu.com
Author Photo: Sarah Collins
Cover Design: Leah Huete

Printed in the USA on acid-free paper.
Order online: www.finishinglinepress.com
　　　　　also available on amazon.com

Author inquiries and mail orders:
Finishing Line Press
P. O. Box 1626
Georgetown, Kentucky 40324
U. S. A.

Table of Contents

Unbelief 1

Body, Post Partum 2

Nullus Partus 3

Translations 5

The Seeker 6

The Rope 7

Working from Home 8

Fruit at Night 10

The Fall 11

An Incomplete Alphabet 12

The Prayer 14

Picking 15

Transplant 16

At the Roadside Rock and Gem Store 17

My Daughter Plays with Water 19

Imsland 21

Snow and Ashes 23

Bean Saving 24

List 25

Thirty 27

Lost Coin 28

Grass 29

Yellow 30

Unbelief

I wait for you the way I wait
for spring—without believing

it will happen. I want to reach land
before I get out of this boat.

So I drift, how long?
Will birds—

sent south and then north again,
then south, inking the gray.

And I can't get the waves
out of my mouth.

Body, Post Partum

        My heart
a mouse
rummaging leaves
for scraps of some
thing I thought
I was.
        My belly
a torn
net, catching
not even breath
in its spent
grasp.
        My child
a snipped yarn
curled just
beyond
reach.
        I am alone
so rarely
and also forever,
and what can I do
        with this

strange flesh
but take it
tender in my hands,
try to soothe
its hunger.

Nullus Partus

I wanted a child
so I took
my temperature
charted mountains
on blue graph squares
compared basin
to crest like a traveler
in a desert landscape
like an architect
on the moon.

I had a child
but she had no bones
he had no sex no name she had
no heartbeat no
birthday.

I tried to imagine
myself without
these things.
I heard a voice
in the night with no
body shaking me who
am I in the night with no
child?

Weight-
less groundless
like an astronaut
at night I dreamed the child
was an astronaut
seeking me seeking
a planet to land on
and every day
she chose someone
else.

I said to the ocean
Jesus if you give me
this I will give you
everything
I have which is
nothing which is endless
like the landscape
inside me.

I dreamed
nothing an ocean
white as sleeplessness
dark as a body
on the inside it was
murky as blood
and I hid in it
and my want
felt like an animal
beside me.

Translations

begin with *gone*

dig a shelter
from the avalanche
of not here, not here

tell me my *sorrow*
with sounds
like sparrow
or wheelbarrow

carry this wing or make it
earthy, make me
a body
I can keep

here, make me
a house inside
death where the walls

won't cave
in, breathe me
a name and speak me
a new

language
watertight enough
to hold me
in

The Seeker

Like the fog of a horse
when it hits your palm,
just before the wet touch
you are afraid of.

Like a sound you don't hear
until it's gone.

Everything is dying—
horse, apple, light, hand.

In my farthest dream,
I am the horse,
coming close
to see who is there.

In the lake of the hallway
there is a door I can open,
into a field blue with dusk:

called in from play, I linger
in the heat rising from the grass,
as if the sun didn't want to leave
the earth. They say

there is one grief
inside of everything.

The Rope

trailed its shadow
through ivy like a snake
in the backyard slope

we took turns falling
over and over
into the sheen of the leaves

though it hurt and we knew it
jabbed sticks and the packed
earth beneath

we wore bruises we touched
scabs we picked and youth
erased them

there was the sky
and the sky
in the tin pan mirror

that one and this one
split, paired
like rope and shadow

Working from Home

> "The Moon and Sun are eternal travelers. Even the years wander on. A lifetime adrift in a boat, or in old age leading a tired horse into the years, every day is a journey, and the journey itself is home."
> Matsuo Basho,
> *Narrow Road to the Interior*

I.

>October
>the Jerusalem artichokes
>finally flower

We arrive in the backyard, in our closets. We are the kind of travelers who nervously pack boiled eggs, who save rubber bands in the silverware drawer. Our clothes never hang right: always the baggy seat of your jeans, the knees worn pale. The wind in my Goodwill blouse, sailing over my small breasts. What is there to celebrate? Why should we mourn? We pause at the lake of the kitchen table, steamed rice fogging your glasses. We tell each other where we have been, what we've seen since breakfast. I shake my head at your bandaged thumbs. Come outside, you say.

II.

>sabi: essential
>aloneness
>no one there

Climbing Moon Mountain, Basho crosses the valley toward Yudono, passing Swordsmith hut. From the garage, your hammer ringing on the anvil. Garbage truck at the curb. Last night I moved the ticking clock from our bedside to the kitchen sill. It kept its tempo, counting down toward dawn, shaving long strips from the wax seal of sky. We woke where we had left ourselves: my ear to your heart, your hand curved to my hip. I put on my shame again like an old cloak. You were already up grinding coffee.

III.

>day moon
>over 84th avenue
>fresh as a wound

To say more is sacrilege, Basho says. But I always say more. There must be more than work, more than the dull thud of the hammer, scrape of the pen. The maple lets down its dinner-plate leaves. Many times, I have almost carried my notebooks to the fire. I say I am glad that is all behind me, but it's still there, this urge for immolation. You make something useful of it—a blade, a ring—heating and shaping the iron. I write it down: there is nowhere to go but here.

Fruit at Night

Like a mother
I fret for you,

little apples
clustered on the bough,

as far south
of the half-ripe moon

as arroyo
from rain.

How can I leave
you, alone

in the branches,
for my soft bed?

You never sleep.
In the morning,

a film of sugar
on your skin

as guiltless
as sweat.

You don't need
my worries,

unskilled, unwilling
to wait through

the night. Already,
you are reaching

toward me.

The Fall

does nobody see?
the split

cedar piled sweet
in the parks

in the jeweled grass
left unguarded

and these two
one body new

and now held
by another: bound

by one cloth
the just-born

just barely
outside the other

once whole
like trees

they swallow the light
skin-first

below giants
the loose leaves

like hands
touching

their shoulders
this one, and this one

An Incomplete Alphabet

> *after "Baby Nursing, Mexico City," by Tina Modotti (b. USA), 1926.*

W-E-
A for ache, an acre, a field of oats

N for new words in your mouth, N for now, for noise: grain in a digital
world, the random optical texture of a photograph, over-
enlarged, exposed

a grainy image: round of cheek to round of breast
a curtain of sleeve, blouse: the round of
earth from space is the round of the baby's
earring, round of her ear

Exposed on park bench, concealed under trees to
enclose you, me:
W-E: light passing between (For
angle, for ache) above the breast, the heart: over-enlarged in
nursing room art: *Dar pecho, un regalo que dura toda una vida*

a pattern just like the original light source
as with seed, Modotti scattered sun onto film

Not giving, this morning: I hear your chair legs
winnow the floor, reaching for spooned oats in your father's hand
W-E- (for grain, for give

forgive me) & you reach
for grain instead, for ache
You cry my name

Pure your gentle name, pure your fragile life
Neruda wrote of Modotti when she died
& gave her a garland of earthly things
to soften her exile: a rosary of *bees, shadows, fire*

Little seed, *pepita, granar*—we lift the leaves in your flip-flap book
"Why do flowers die?"
Because they are no longer needed

In the photograph, the baby's mouth
blossoms over the mother's breast

round as earth from far away

The Prayer

The ants know something.
Each one carries work,
whether it fits
in a lifetime
or not.
        They are manyness
scrawled across black
plastic tubing, bodies
barely revealed
by sun.
        As for me, I'm in love
with guarantee,
with germination
rates, five-year warranties.
I cuss and wrestle
the trimmer, its pile
of broken teeth.
        Bees
make early rounds.
Frogs consult tomes
of spinach. The cherries
and plums will take
March or June, give
their blossom hearts over
to spring.
        I try to wrest
mercy from the ground
like a turnip, make it grow
with my own red hands. I can't
take this birdsong, this waltz
of insect and sunflower, each
nodding head a *yes*
that breaks apart.

Picking

Cold dirt turned over
in the morning dark.

Moving quiet in the carrot field,
the boggy lowers that will flood
come November.

I measure myself
in bundles of rainbow chard,
pushing down hard
so the stems snap clean.

White hands puckered red,
I stack and bend,
strip the spent leaves
plant by plant down the row,
making room for the next
to grow in. I need

to be here, learning
a language of leaves.
The sealed boats of Little Gem.
The silence of Deer's Tongue.
Sweet Jericho, shoulders held
upright. I want each
head of lettuce
to count.

Transplant

The city trucks came pollarding.
I watched the saws
treat all the trees the same.

Our house flattened with the rest,
grove of avocado making way
for megaliths on concrete pads.
So close nothing but shadows
fit between them.

Bitter as the oleander
in the freeway median,
I left my native home
to raze itself.

I carried with me common names
for what I found uncommon—
honeysuckle, catmint, Mexican poppy—
and cuttings from the bank of Cymbidium
in our backyard.

They paled and died
in the gray light up north.
Moss grows on sidewalks here.
Rain spills like change
from great pockets.

Still my skin resists,
the way abandoned soil
forgets its love of water.

At the Roadside Rock and Gem Store

In the windowless
room, we plunge knuckle-
deep into agate

I peer through shards
of peridot, and you
say *choose*.

Here are citrine,
banded rhyolite, a mellow
violence of serpentine.

Here the tiger's eye
and its deceit, glinting
silk inside the bin

and lesser quartz
locked in display,
exposed. No,

not tourmaline, that candy
melon. I might
place a wheel of it

as wafer on my tongue.
No crust goes down
easy with me.

I want nothing
to do with this skull,
back in the cases

of petrified logs and ambered
insects, leaves denied
the sleep of dissolution.

Say this isn't me
buried alive
in my body.

I want a rock
older than earth.
Side by side

in the mirror, the cold gaze
of halite and gypsum.
Then I find it—a scene

dug from a desert wall,
a human figure there
in the rock, as sure

as the beetles
and gelled mosquitos,
there all along, waiting

at the mute core
to be known. Or not—
that's the discovery

I make, the rock
I choose—this raised
and hidden body.

My Daughter Plays with Water

I want to see and feel it
as she does: a column
of somethingness
pierceable, not stopped;
touchable, not kept.

On and on
out of the green
hose it goes and I
shouldn't let her— should twist
the spigot back to August
swelter, acquiesce
to the spider
hanging around just there,
who wants a little closer
to coolness—

but I want the water, too
its kindness and colorless hair
slendering out between concrete
and gate and slip-sliding
tell-tale downstreet
(surely the neighbors

must think) but just now
let me this once
not think
of bureau bills, of fire
picking tree meat
from coast-bones
down south
where drought
is a miser,
coughing dust
at gone lawns,

of children like her
who need years of this
clean, healing stuff—
and maybe the same fate
awaits us, so now

I want to just see it,
what she sees: nothing
but thoroughly
something, clear
as a mirror and just
as misleading.

Imsland

> *for Lyle*

In the churchyard,
the stones lean over, grown tired
of repeating the name.

The plain line
of the grass farmer's mouth
never ripples, as he takes a key
from his pocket, unlocks

the church for you
unasked. Love, you sit
in the pew, in the town

the name came from,
as if to return
something borrowed.

What else could you bring
from California to Oslo,
from tunnel to tunnel

to Imsland, through mile
after empty mile of snow?
The name is a common mirror

here, seaming man to man
as the fjord links earth to sky.
As the sheep follow you

from the church to the inn,
you trail a ghost here, hoping
a shadow might linger in land

as in language. In the end,
you'll leave as your ancestor left:
alone, called by all he had lost.

Backward like salmon
toward the scent of home,
one that knows you by name.

Snow and Ashes

In the graveyard,
the snow softens the stones
while we walk, idle talk about how
we'll be buried.

You want to live forever
in the canyon we love,
your skin and bone
become sugar pine
and chaparral.

Snowflakes catch
and thread my hair,
melt in the heat of my hands.

You're no more mine
than the thousand seeds
winging down yearly
around the cabin,
each one a try for roothold
on a hillside in the sun.

Even now you are leaving me,
here in my body
with my envy of trees.

Bean Saving

Outside, the garden black,
burlap tossed back from beds
as if from fevered sleep.

Rain comes down and rain
comes down. The beans
leave their pale circles
inside the husk, like the white
behind my wedding ring.

We tell each other again
about the trellised vines
how they climbed all seven rungs
and when they reached air
kept going, lacing together
like fingers, getting closer
to the sun. The dark

comes early, winter falling down
around us. In last year's snow
I thought I'd be spent
come October, broken open
and provident as earth.

I shake with it—this sensible
putting away,
these sketches
of next year's garden.

List

The gray wakes on my chest
I'm alive, I breathe
the gas tank's full, the sun
shines, our daughter's
head reaches
the silverware drawer.

The book is unfinished
I am brushing
my teeth, another empty room
I am alive, the machine gargling
in the laundry room.

The bill is paid, an hour
is filled, my hands, two sieves
the cat asleep
in a box, the mind
lies, the bed
we shared last night
a juice cup, your key
in the lock, her
belly laugh, I am alive.

My face
twitches, the tree
drops pears on the lawn
obituaries are read, pencils
sharpened, entire
calendars
crossed out.

My heart
pours water, the neighbor
smiles, the war, the child
at the park, I am thinking
of making lasagna, the car
is fixed, I am alive, noise
from a radio, an unborn baby
not crying, a ladybug lands
on the windshield, your hands
startle behind glass.

Thirty

We drink tea in the sunroom
cupped to the side of your building
like a shell to an ear.

Across the alley, an identical room.
Your neighbor watering her orchids.

Did Baudelaire say life is a hospital?

It turns out we want
what our parents had:
some kind of brightness
we can afford.

An amaryllis in the corner,
stout as a boxer.
Not to admit defeat.

It turns out life is a will,
an overfed bulb
that can be forced to bloom again
and again.

Lost Coin

Another morning

in last night's clothes.
I cling to the silver pole

while the Metro rocks
and I look at no one.

A look is a danger.
Out comes the soul, leaking

secrets. Last time
it disappeared into the crowds

underground. I wandered
the tunnels for hours, calling.

Here is a coin of no recognizable value.
My soul collects

this sort of thing. I cannot keep it
in. It returns to me the way

it pours out,
obedient as milk.

Grass

Once we fell asleep
in the meadow
during a meteor shower,
wind licking our thoughts so
they knelt like blades.

Another night I lay staring
up from bare ground until
I saw one fall—*Hello*—
and I knew I was going
out like that, and you were
an orange glow in the window
washing dishes, tinning
silver on ceramic and then

there, breaking the dark
like a yolk and saying
should I get a blanket?

Tuesday morning, I passed
a couple asleep
beneath a row of cypress
trees— new, and clear of words
they didn't mean

and I remembered I told you
No, meaning *blanket*
meaning you in the grass
with me covered in stars,
but you were already gone.

Yellow

I am making you a kimono,
yellow as the ordinary things of the world
you do not know. There are dandelions

here, sunlight on the butter dish.
There is melting, and gold,
and cling peaches in juice.

You move now freer than I am:
naked and weightless, swimming.
I am making you clothes, though

they bother me: tags and edges,
buttons and zippers keeping me in.
They say this dress

will make things easy
when you're new. Open and fold,
snap, snap, you're ready—yellow

as a young duck, a phone book,
the creek after rain. The yellow
of canary and caution. Slow down.

The birth that waits for you is real
as a lemon or leaf, hard
as the soap on the sink ledge.

I am pressing out seams, wanting
to soften the blow. Picturing
rupture and light tearing in,

torrents of sound. The everyday walls
leaning toward you. So many things
I can't explain. Subtractive, starting

with light. Most visible color. The yellow
of Judas, yellow stars, yellowcake.
I am sewing so slowly.

Notes

"Working from Home"
Quotation is from Matsuo Basho's *Narrow Road to the Interior,* translated by Sam Hamill.

"An Incomplete Alphabet"
Quotation is from Pablo Neruda's epitaph for Tina Modotti, engraved on her tombstone:

> "Pure your gentle name, pure your fragile life,
> bees, shadows, fire, snow, silence and foam,
> combined with steel and wire and
> pollen to make up your firm
> and delicate being."

Additional Acknowledgements

I would like to thank everyone at Finishing Line Press for your care in publishing this book. To my mentors, Jeanine Hathaway and Jeanne Murray Walker, and my extended MFA family, thank you for growing me up as a poet. Thank you Deb Conkey, Noel Tendick, Veronica Golos, Claudia Savage, Jill McKenna, Cheryl Wallick, Jo Vance, Adie Smith, and Jess Gigot for the role each of you played in shaping these poems and bringing this book into being. Thank you to my writing group, Caitlin, Emily, Kaitlin, Renee, and Stephanie, for inspiring and encouraging me. You have my deepest admiration. To my sister Autumn, for the fierceness of your friendship, and to my parents, Tom and Kim, for fostering creativity in us from the beginning. And to my own constellation, Lyle, Sky, and Robin: I love you immeasurably.

Melissa Reeser Poulin is a poet and writer. A graduate of Seattle Pacific University's MFA program, she was the winner of the 2016 Janet B. McCabe Poetry Prize. She is the editor, along with Jill McKenna, of *Winged: New Writing on Bees* (Poulin Publishing, 2014), an anthology on the relationship between humans and honeybees, benefitting pollinator conservation. She was formerly a teacher of creative writing and managing editor of *Boneshaker: A Bicycling Almanac*, the thinking person's literary bicycle-themed periodical. Her most recent poems, essays, and articles appear in *Relief Journal, Red Tricycle, Ruminate Magazine, Coffee + Crumbs, Hip Mama,* and *In Good Tilth*. She lives in Portland, Oregon with her husband and two children. melissareeserpoulin.com

www.ingramcontent.com/pod-product-compliance
Lightning Source LLC
LaVergne TN
LVHW041603070426
835507LV00011B/1280